T0130050

Behind Leah's Veil

Darlene Vice

authorHOUSE®

AuthorHouse™
1663 Liberty Drive
Bloomington, IN 47403
www.authorhouse.com
Phone: 1 (800) 839-8640

© *2019 Darlene Vice. All rights reserved.*

No part of this book may be reproduced, stored in a retrieval system, or transmitted by any means without the written permission of the author.

Published by AuthorHouse 12/18/2018

ISBN: 978-1-5462-7312-7 (sc)
ISBN: 978-1-5462-7313-4 (hc)
ISBN: 978-1-5462-7311-0 (e)

Library of Congress Control Number: 2018914975

Print information available on the last page.

Any people depicted in stock imagery provided by Getty Images are models, and such images are being used for illustrative purposes only.
Certain stock imagery © Getty Images.

This book is printed on acid-free paper.

Because of the dynamic nature of the Internet, any web addresses or links contained in this book may have changed since publication and may no longer be valid. The views expressed in this work are solely those of the author and do not necessarily reflect the views of the publisher, and the publisher hereby disclaims any responsibility for them.

Scripture quotations marked NKJV are taken from the New King James Version. Copyright © 1982 by Thomas Nelson, Inc. Used by permission. All rights reserved.

To my mother,
the one who introduced me to Jesus

CONTENTS

Once upon a time … don't we all just love that opening line of a story? The little girl in us just smiles and giggles and anticipates a wonderful story where the good guys will win, the girl's favorite guy falls in love with her, and everybody lives happily ever after. Don't you wish life was really like that? Don't you wish that everything would always fall right into place and all your dreams come true at the very moment you choose? Of all the promises in the Bible, a fairy tale life is not one of them. But here's the good news: God has an awesome plan for each of us. And, hopefully, all of us will find some measure of happily ever after that will come by following God's leading and instruction.

When I first became the director of Women's Ministry at our local church in Alabama, God immediately began to stir my heart with compassion for the emotional state of women. Perhaps it came from working in public health for more than a decade and seeing firsthand women whose lives had literally been shattered for whatever reason, women who lived in fear, women who had nothing to feed their children, and teenage women looking for love in all the wrong places. I've known women that had no identity and hovered in a corner after being beaten down. My heart aches for the women of today. The members of our women's group that I direct will tell you that my main goal is emotional healing for women, and my message to every woman is that you are beautiful, and you are loved. One of our recent themes for the year was simply "Live" from Psalms 116:9: "I will walk before the Lord in the land of the living" (NKJV). So many women just exist. They don't live.

In *Behind Leah's Veil* we will examine the emotional state of Leah, as well as Rachel, and perhaps we will be able to see a little bit of ourselves. And maybe, just maybe, we can rewrite our own stories. Maybe something like "Once upon a time there was a woman named _____. She met a prince named Jesus, and they lived happily ever after."

Go with me now to Haran where a couple of sisters wait for their princes to come, to see what God has in store for their lives. They had no idea that they had been handpicked for a purpose that would change the world for every generation.

CHAPTER 1

Assumptions

"Finally, brethren, whatever things are true, whatever things are noble, whatever things are just, whatever things are pure, whatever things are lovely, whatever things are of good report, if there is any virtue and if there is anything praiseworthy—meditate on these things" (Philippians 4:8 NKJV). There are so many reasons God gave us this scripture. Notice the very first criteria of the things we're cautioned to think about—whatever things are true.

I once had a coworker whose greatest advice was to never assume anything. I learned that the hard way. It's so much easier to assume that something is this way or that way, that we understand exactly what it is, and that we are fully aware of all the details and are perfectly capable of making a decision. You have no idea how many errors I've had to correct in my lifetime because I made an assumption that was completely wrong. The very definition of assumption, according to Webster's, is something that is believed to be true or probably true but that is not known to be true. God does not deal in lies or half-truths. Assumptions are based on half-truths, lies, and human perception. Can I confess something else? Sometimes I've made the wrong assumption about people. Most people never consider that they don't know all the facts, have not heard everybody's stories, are completely unaware of other factors involved in a particular situation, and draw conclusions based on what they think they know. Unfortunately, most of the time assumptions are totally wrong. It's been my experience that there are far more situations that I never know all the facts than those situations where I do. It's also been my experience that assumptions close the mind to any possibility other than what we have decided. Actually, the only situations that I know everything about are my own. Chances are it's the same for everyone. Over the last few years God has really pricked my heart about assumptions, especially when it comes to people. Many reputations have been ruined and marriages and families torn apart or suffered some way because of assumptions. Assumption leads to judgment. And judgment leads to disaster. I guess that's why God led me to include this section first. Now, the Bible doesn't always give details, and we sometimes don't have a choice but to assume and try to fill in the blanks, but as I began this study, I noticed that my mind automatically made assumptions about each character involved in our story. I have to admit I was quite taken by surprise to realize that everything I thought I knew was an assumption. I've heard this story my whole life, so I have all the facts, right? I started to jot down all the assumptions I've been making for more than five decades. So, for just a little while, let's step away from assumptions, identify the things we think we know, broaden the possibilities in our minds, and get reacquainted with Leah, Rachel, and Jacob.

Leah

Our biggest assumption about Leah is that she suffers from some deformity with her eyes. Was she cross-eyed, or was it a lazy eye? King James just calls it "weak." Other versions call it "tender." Nevertheless, the one fact we know is that there is some kind of issue with the eyes. I ran across some interesting opinions concerning Leah's eyes. Some seem to believe she was simply very timid, so eye contact was not a strong point. Others blame allergies due to the sand and climate that caused her eyes to be red and watery. But here's the most interesting one—the Torah states that because of custom, Leah knew she was supposed to marry one of Rebecca's sons, and since she was the oldest daughter, she would most likely be given to the oldest son, Esau. The Torah further states that Leah had heard many things about Esau and knew that he did not follow the Lord's commandments and that she was so heartbroken over the thought of becoming the wife of a man like him that she wept constantly so that her eyes were always red and swollen. Whatever the reason, this one detail in the Bible about her eyes causes us to assume that she was completely unattractive, even just plain ugly, and that her eyes alone were to blame for her unmarried state. Bless her. If the Lord had decided to include me like He did Leah, I wonder how many columns in the Bible it would take to list all of my physical flaws. And I don't think that this detail is included in the Word of God to be mean; it's included to let us know that judging people on their physical appearances is not new to our day. It's been human nature for centuries.

Jacob

Jacob was a mama's boy—that's not an assumption—and his mother had instructed him to go to the house of her brother, Laban, to get him away from Esau after the birthright deception. The assumption we make is that he arrived in Haran, met Rachel, fell madly in love with her, and the love story unfolds from there. We make this assumption because while we remember that his mother was truly trying to save his life by sending him there, she also instructed him to take a wife from Laban's daughters. Therefore, we have to keep in mind that he *intended* to marry one of them. Now, scripture specifically tells us that he really did see Rachel first, and he really did fall in love with her. But there is nothing to tell us that he knew which one he would marry before he arrived or that he even expected to truly love one of them. Maybe love was a bonus, an unexpected blessing. Nevertheless, in order to get a good, clear picture of this whole story, we have to remember that he planned to marry, love or not. Lucky for him he met the girl of his dreams and was smitten.

There is one other assumption we make about Jacob that I'm not sure has any merit. We assume he didn't love Leah at all. Just go with me for a minute here. Genesis 29:30 says he loved Rachel *more* than Leah. "Then Jacob also went in to Rachel, and he also loved Rachel more than Leah" (NKJV). Let's keep in mind that he had several babies with Leah, so is it too much of an assumption to say that he had some sort of affection for her? Obviously, he spent a little time with her and obviously her "weak" eye was not an issue. We'll get into some deeper emotions about the wedding morning reveal in a few more chapters, but for right now, let's just try to keep in mind that even though he was in love with Rachel and that Operation Bride Switch had to send him for a loop, it doesn't mean that he wasn't friends with Leah, that he didn't like her at all, or that he wanted to hurt her. After all, she was family. She was his cousin and the sister of the woman he loved.

Rachel

Rachel, the fair maiden, the favored, beautiful one. It is believed by most Bible scholars that her personality was outgoing, lively, and very likable—all in addition to being extremely attractive. My assumption of Rachel is that she must have been cocky and conceited. What's up with that? Where did I get that? And perhaps she was! But we have nothing to indicate that, so it's not fair to her to assume the worst just because she was pretty, got all of the attention, and everybody would rather hang out with her than her sister. Sorry, Rachel.

You know what else I've always assumed about Rachel? I've always assumed that she was in love with Jacob. What scripture tells me that? I don't even find where she had a choice in the matter. Fast forward for a moment to Genesis 31:15. Laban has once again cheated Jacob over the livestock, and Jacob is ready to take his wives and his children and settle someplace far away from his father-in-law. To help him make the decision, he calls both Rachel and Leah to discuss the matter and get their take on it. That's one point for Jacob, since most men in that culture in that day wouldn't have considered a woman's point of view. Both sisters agree that "dad sold us." Look at verse 15: "Are we not considered strangers by him? For he has sold us, and also completely consumed our money" (NKJV). Hmmmmm. Is it right, then, to assume that Rachel loved Jacob as much as he loved her? After all, Jacob asked Laban for her and negotiated a bride price or dowry for her. She had no choice but to marry him. She had no choice in Operation Bride Switch either. We know that God had this all planned out, but she hadn't read the rest of the story and didn't have a clue how it would end. Hopefully, she loved him too, but it reminds me of Romans 8:28: "And we know that all things work together for good to those who love God, to those who are the called according to His purpose" (NKJV). Aren't you glad for that, sisters? No matter what situation or circumstance you find yourself in, and no matter how you got there, whether through your own choices or someone else's, God knew about it when he planned your very existence. He had already figured it into His plan for your life and knew exactly how He was going to make it work. There is no sin, no mistake, no choice you make that surprises God and that diminishes the awesome plan He has for you. I love that!

Now on that note, let's move on a little further.

Challenge Question #1

Have you ever made an assumption about someone? Were you correct? Who was it, and what was right and wrong about your conclusions?

_____

_____

_____

_____

_____

_____

_____

_____

_____

_____

_____

_____

_____

_____

_____

_____

_____

_____

_____

_____

_____

Challenge Question #2

Has anyone ever made an assumption about you? How did it make you feel, and what was your reaction?

_____

_____

_____

_____

_____

_____

_____

_____

_____

_____

_____

_____

_____

_____

_____

_____

_____

_____

_____

_____

_____

_____

_____

Journal

CHAPTER 2

Operation Bride Switch

I'm intrigued by biblical customs, so I've studied enough about weddings to know that there are so many elements that simply do not make sense. Maybe I'm just too curious, but I have so many questions. Like, did Rachel and Leah know what dear old dad had planned, or did he just spring it on them when it was time for the bride to go to the bedroom? If Rachel did know, then did she participate as the bride all the days of the wedding festivities and then just hand over her groom at the last minute? And if it was exactly that way, how did she keep her emotions under control? Or did she not want to marry him and was happy to trade places with her sister? If Leah knew, was she excited, or did she dread the switch? Was she jealous that Rachel got all the bridal attention during the celebration? And did Laban consider the feelings of his daughters at all, or was it all just a way to get some free labor for several more years? The questions go on and on, and the worst part about is that I don't have an answer for a single one of them. And since we've already established the danger of assumptions, we can't just start trying to make up answers.

But I know this just as sure as I know that the world spins—Leah was shattered. It doesn't matter when this scheme devised by Laban was brought to her attention. Prior knowledge, last minute surprise—it's irrelevant when we really go behind her veil to the real girl, to the raw emotions that she experienced on the morning after her wedding.

Let's get a clear picture. Jacob rides into town on a white horse … well, okay, he slides into town on the run from his brother, and the first person he meets is Rachel. Beautiful, lively, full-of-life Rachel. How did that compare when he met shy Leah? Wasn't she used to being in her sister's shadow? Always in the background. Always the one no one noticed. We have no idea how Leah felt about Jacob, but she watched him fall in love with Rachel. She knew about the seven-year contract between Jacob and Laban, and she knew as they planned the wedding for them that Jacob fully expected his bride to be Rachel.

Can you imagine the dread she had for the morning after when the veil would come off, and Jacob would know of the deceit? Don't you think she dreaded seeing the look in his eyes upon finding her in his bed instead of Rachel? First shock, then disappointment, and then anger. My heart goes out to her. Now in his defense, I can't tell you what kind of reaction I would have had on the morning after my wedding if I had discovered that the man I thought was my husband was someone else. I honestly don't think I would have done well. So I'm sure it was impossible for Jacob to hide those emotions after such a revelation too. It would take some time to process what just happened! But that doesn't change the fact that Leah's heart shattered to pieces. No doubt she sat there in shame. All night long she listened to him whisper the name of the woman he loved, the one who truly held his heart. But it wasn't her name. He didn't choose her, didn't love her, and didn't want her. And all she wanted was to be loved. I wonder if it would have made a difference if Laban had been honest in the beginning and simply told Jacob that Leah had to marry first. Would Jacob have agreed? He still wouldn't love her, but at least it wouldn't have been deceit. And maybe, just maybe, he would have called Leah's name through their first night together. But she would never know. Married less than twenty-four hours and already Leah knew he would never be happy with her. She was not enough. Less than twenty-four hours, and her husband had already gone to Laban and negotiated a new contract for another woman.

My heart goes out to Leah. And my heart goes out to many of you who have experienced these same emotions that Leah did. You were not the chosen one and were told that you were not enough. You've been told you're not pretty enough, not slim enough, not smart enough, not _____ (you fill in the blank). And not just by a man, either. These daggers were thrown at you from other people in your life. Mom, dad, brother, sister, classmates … I asked God for a scripture for you, sister, to let you know that, for God, you *are* enough. All I could think about was Isaiah 43:1–2: "But now, thus says the Lord, who created you, O Jacob, And He who formed you, O Israel: Fear not, for I have redeemed you; I have called you by your name; You are Mine. When you pass through the waters, I will be with you; And through the rivers, they shall not overflow you. When you walk through the fire, you shall not be burned, Nor shall the flame scorch you" (NKJV). Doesn't every woman long for the man that will love her unconditionally, that will be true to her, that turns to no other, that walks through every circumstance with her, and that will give his very life for her? You have that man. The love of no earthly man will ever come close to the love that Jesus has for you. No earthly love will ever satisfy the way He can. But you have to accept it, and let Him be enough for you. If you're waiting for a man who is willing to give his life for you, well, Jesus isn't just willing; he already has.

CHAPTER 3

Maternity Race

You are probably aware that in that culture in that time, the absolute most important thing for both men and women was children. A man wasn't truly considered a man unless he could father children. And not just a child but a boy. Girls were not considered valuable except as free labor, for what bride price she could bring to her father, and for her ability to give some man a male child. It stands to reason, then, that any woman who could not bear children was a complete disgrace to her husband. Hence, this maternity race between the sisters.

Everything about this whole situation was completely backward from the norm. What was supposed to happen was the father of the bride and the groom negotiated some sort of dowry and/or bride price, the wedding happened, and the new Mrs. leaves her father's household and joins her husband's. But in this case, Jacob didn't have anything to offer, and he couldn't go back to his father's household. Laban took advantage of that and saw a farmhand for at least seven years, and if he could maneuver everything just right, he might be able to extend that to fourteen years. And so it happened just that way.

But Jacob finally got his girl, and Leah faded into the background. Obviously, God didn't like that, since Genesis 29:31 tells us: "When the Lord saw that Leah was unloved, He opened her womb; but Rachel was barren" (NKJV). Despite the fact that Leah was not as pretty as Rachel, and Jacob didn't love her like he did Rachel, she still had six boys and one girl by him. Again, remember if we were making assumptions, we would assume that whatever physical flaws Leah had were of very little concern for Jacob since he obviously spent some time with her. His firstborn just happened to be a boy, so, thankfully, Jacob was able to prove he was a real man. That child was born to him by Leah. She named him Reuben, which, according to Genesis 29:32, means, "The Lord has surely looked on my affliction. Now therefore, my husband will love me" (NKJV). Bless her. All she wanted was to be loved by her husband. Is that too much to ask? Granted, she was part a deceptive scheme, but remember that girls were not considered valuable and must be obedient to their fathers and then to their husbands with very little voice in any matter. She only did as instructed by dear old dad, who seemed to only be interested in the free labor by Jacob. Again, my heart goes out to her. She gave him the one thing that all Jewish men want—a son. And he still didn't love her like she longed for.

Simeon. Son #2 born to Jacob by Leah. "Then she conceived again and bore a son, and said, 'Because the Lord has heard that I am unloved, He has therefore given me this son also.' And she called his name Simeon" (Genesis 29:33 NKJV). And then came Levi. "She conceived again and bore a son, and said, 'Now this time my husband will become attached to me, because I have borne him three sons.' Therefore his name was called Levi" (Genesis 29:34 NKJV).

Leah is three sons ahead of Rachel, and with every baby she has desperately hoped that this time this son will win Jacob over, even choosing names that echo the desperate cry of her heart. And Jacob never picked up on this? But what a change with the next son!

"And she conceived again and bore a son, and said, 'Now I will praise the Lord.' Therefore she called his name Judah. Then she stopped bearing" (Genesis 29:35 NKJV).

After all this time of trying to win Jacob's affection and his love, after all the sons she had borne to him, after every name of every son referred to this longing, this desire to be loved by Jacob, this fourth son was different. She finally just stops it all and says, "Hey, you know what? I'm done trying to win Jacob. I'm just gonna praise the Lord." Oh, sisters, this is the absolute meat of this whole study. If you don't get anything else, pay attention right here. With this surrender, everything changed. Judah. Out of Judah would come a Messiah! This Messiah would be called the Lion of Judah, and his sacrifice would conquer sin, death, hell, and the grave, and pave the way for every man, woman, and child for every generation to receive eternal life! Out of Leah's praise came a promise! Many times, sweet sisters, we try over and over; we struggle, and we weep over circumstances. But it's your praise that releases your promise! Not just any praise but praise that comes from a truly surrendered heart.

Challenge Question

Are you hiding behind a veil? Can you identify with any of the emotions that Leah experienced?

_____

_____

_____

_____

_____

_____

_____

_____

_____

_____

_____

_____

_____

_____

_____

_____

_____

_____

_____

_____

Journal

_____

_____

_____

_____

_____

_____

_____

_____

_____

_____

_____

_____

_____

_____

_____

_____

_____

_____

_____

_____

_____

_____

_____

_____

Darlene Vice

CHAPTER 4

No Rocks

"But He answered and said to them, 'I tell you that if these should keep silent, the stones would immediately cry out'" (Luke 19:40 NKJV). Before we go any further in defining the characteristics of a surrendered heart, of praise let's establish the difference between praise and worship. We often use them in the same sentence and frequently refer to the "praise and worship" service at church. I have served as worship leader, and some of my greatest moments came from a praise and worship service. But if you always limit your praise and your worship to a gathering of other Christians, you are missing it!

It is very difficult to possess a heart of praise if you don't first live a lifestyle of worship. I ran across a quote by William Temple where he defines worship. He says "to worship is to quicken the conscience by the holiness of God, to feed the mind with the truth of God, to purge the imagination by the beauty of God, to open the heart to the love of God, to devote the will to the purpose of God." Worship is an everyday thing. It's being committed to focus solely on God and living out His commandments. Worship is not something we do; it's something we live. It becomes our top priority. When we come to the place where we see God for who He is, a lifestyle of worship should be a natural response.

Praise is bragging on God. It's letting Him know how much He means to us and expresses our admiration of Him to Him. If you live a lifestyle of worship, it is impossible not to praise. You can't help it. Words of adoration and love for God just spill over and out of your mouth. That's when the praise and worship service when we gather becomes a celebration. It's a result of the lifestyle of worship we've been living all week. We can't help but sing to the top of our lungs, to raise our hands, and even to give in the offering (yes, that's part of worship). Having said that, let me gently say this: if a worship leader, a pastor, or other person in charge has to coax you into singing, raising your hands, giving in the offering or whatever way your church worships, then you might want to take a moment and examine yourself. I will be the first to admit that we go through things that cause us to feel anything but celebratory. But true praise and true worship has nothing to do with feelings or any battle we are going through. Celebration of our relationship with God doesn't have to be loud; it's not in the dance or hype in music or whatever it is you do when you gather with your group. Some of the most awesome moments I have ever spent with God were kneeling at His feet in silence with tears running down my face. It's not the form; it's the heart. A true heart of praise that has been developed from a true lifestyle of worship enables us to tell God how much we love Him even in the midst of the hardest battle.

In a later chapter I'll talk a little about being presence-minded. Worship is a vital key. True worship will bring you to a place where you can focus on God rather than your circumstances, and prepare your heart to receive the Word of God. The benefits of a lifestyle of worship and a heart of praise are endless.

Please don't limit your time of praise and worship to a Sunday morning church service. God will meet you on Sunday but wants you to know that He's waiting for you on Monday morning too. And Tuesday, and Wednesday …

Challenge Question

Is your praise to God the result of a daily lifestyle of worship, or is it just weekly words of lip service?

_____

_____

_____

_____

_____

_____

_____

_____

_____

_____

_____

_____

_____

_____

_____

_____

_____

_____

_____

_____

_____

_____

_____

_____

Journal

_____

_____

_____

_____

_____

_____

_____

_____

_____

_____

_____

_____

_____

_____

_____

_____

_____

_____

_____

_____

_____

_____

_____

_____

_____

_____

_____

_____

_____

_____

_____

_____

_____

_____

_____

_____

_____

_____

_____

_____

_____

_____

_____

_____

_____

_____

_____

_____

CHAPTER 5

Trust/Trustworthy

"Trust in the LORD with all your heart, and lean not on your own understanding; in all your ways acknowledge Him, And He shall direct your paths" Proverbs 3:5-6 (NKJV).

The surrendered heart of praise is one that trusts. By definition, trust refers to belief in the reliability, honesty, truth, and strength of another person. Trust is one of those things that is extremely strong and extremely delicate at the same time. A relationship that is based on trust—whether it's marriage, friendship, business … whatever—will prosper because the goals are generally the same, love is present, and they are walking the same path of life side by side. But trust is only one decision away from being broken. And once broken, it is beyond difficult to earn back. Now we have to remember that God is a miracle worker and through grace and forgiveness can restore that which we believe is beyond repair. But trust is a great treasure given to each individual, and both the person giving it and the person receiving it must handle with care. There are people all around us, both men and women of all ages, who are afraid to trust. The broken marriage vows destroy the trust in a husband or wife, the little girl who is abused by a man refuses to trust all men, the little boy abused by a woman loses trust in all women, and a child abused by both men and women grows up believing there is no one on the face of the planet that can be trusted. What's scarier than being a child and having no one to turn to?

It's an honor when someone places his/her trust in you and then trusts you to be worthy of it. The husband and wife must live a married life beyond the wedding ceremony; Mom and Dad must step up to be providers, protectors, and the ones who love unconditionally after the birth. Get the picture? Can we take it up a level and realize that salvation is the same? One must live a saved life after the salvation experience. That leads to the next question. Can God trust you?

Don't you think that God's trust is also a great treasure to Him, and He wants to know that the person He gives it to will walk worthy of it? We spend so much time worried about our own trust in God. We constantly ask for prayer so we can trust God more for this and more for that, and it's all about us trying to trust that God will do what we want Him to. Newsflash. It's not all about you. It's not all about trying to trust more that God will answer your prayer exactly the way you have asked so you won't have to scream, "Why, God? I trusted you," and be able to justify your anger when He chooses something different. I confess that I've been there. If you haven't, then you're doing much better than I am. If we can recognize that trust is a two-way street between us and other people because you give your trust and receive trust in return, then why don't we recognize that it's still a two-way street when it comes to God?

God dropped this revelation like a ton of bricks on me a few years ago during a Wednesday night class that I was preparing to teach. It was on the old story of the crossing of the Red Sea. It amazes me how I can read something for decades and then all of a sudden see a brand new nugget that I've never seen before. (I love it when God does that!) Have you ever noticed that right after God tells the Israelites to go forward that the cloud of the Lord moved and went behind them? These people had been walking engulfed in the presence of God in a very unique way, and then at the scariest moment, when the enemy is just about to overtake them, that presence moved. They're looking at water and have been told to be ready to march. The Bible plainly says that God just moved behind them. He didn't leave; He just moved in a different way than they were used to. But you know what He had to do? He had to trust them to obey the marching orders that He had given. There's a great truth here! It's not likely that God will ever give you the big picture. That wouldn't require any trust or faith, would it? Right now you may be "looking at water" and wondering where God is. He hasn't left you, sis. He's just moving in a different way than you are used to. But God is trusting you to listen for the marching orders and to move without hesitation when He gives the signal. No matter what's in front of you, take a step of faith! God is looking for a people he can trust to follow Him. He's looking for a people that will move in faith without question and with total abandon regardless of any circumstance or enemy presence. You know what God knew that they didn't? He knew that Jericho was coming. And He knew that they would have to go through Jericho before they could receive their promise. Was the Red Sea a test, perhaps? Was God looking for the remnant that would refrain from grumbling and murmuring and just trust and obey? Only a remnant from that group that crossed the Red Sea made it to the Promised Land, you know. If God couldn't trust them at the beginning of the journey to take a simple step when He said to, then how could He trust them in the heat of the battle in Jericho with a weapon in their hand? Here's another newsflash: Jericho is coming. It's coming in our individual lives, and it's coming as a whole to the people of God.

I have to admit that after this revelation, I began to wonder how many times I had failed the trustworthiness test. How many times had I delayed my miracle or missed my blessing or missed an opportunity? It is a sobering thought that I might not have been part of the remnant that made it to the Promised Land. And all because I was too scared to move. So I stood still in disobedience and held on to my fear, indecision, frustration, and despair looking at the water wondering where God went. And all along God knew that I could be free. But I had to take a step and release it all to Him.

Release. Personally, release is one of my greatest struggles. By definition it means to allow or enable to escape from confinement or set free. I'm a fixer. I believe that I can and should fix every situation for everybody. This belief has absolutely no biblical basis, but I live by it every day without fail. And if I can't figure out how to fix it, I become overwhelmed with guilt.

I will never forget the words my daughter spoke to me concerning some issues that she was facing. After spending a lot of energy trying to find a solution, she looked at me and simply said, "Mom, you can't fix this." I sat there for a few seconds in utter disbelief that she didn't believe in my ability to rescue her. My heart sank and a feeling of helplessness seemed to engulf me. Her words of truth shot holes all in my theory that I was perfectly capable of finding a solution, but her words were just that—truth.

There was no condemnation for my inability to help her. She didn't hold it against me. Her only expectation was that I would pray for her as she found her own way. I never told her what an eye-opening moment that was for me, but the truth she spoke that day still echoes loud and clear.

Most of you can relate because you are a fixer too. You also live daily by the compelling, overwhelming, yet unbiblical belief that you can and should fix whatever it is that touches your family. Where is it written that it's all up to you? Where is it written that it's your responsibility to make sure the world keeps spinning?

I've come to realize, at least in my own life, that many times I'm really praying for *relief* from circumstances. I just want to breathe easier. It's like taking medicine for the flu so you can feel better, but you've only treated a symptom. You still have the flu. God is not interested in your *relief* as much as He is interested in your complete *release* of the whole situation. Release brings a whole new level of trust. You're finally able to acknowledge God's sovereignty, and you realize that no matter what happens, it is what God believes is best for you. God will never settle for anything less than what is your absolute best.

I'm not going to tell you release is easy; nor am I going to tell you how to do it. Mainly because I really have no idea. Frankly, if I knew how, then this last section would read completely different. I would simply give you the steps, and we would all live tomorrow guilt free because we can't fix something. But I know this. God instructs us in 1 Peter 5:7: "casting all your care upon Him, for He cares for you" (NKJV). That's release. Whatever you're holding on to is safer in His hands than in your grip. He's the fixer. When you get to the end of all your possibles, He can do the impossible.

Let's look back at Proverbs 3:5–6. "Trust in the LORD with all your heart, and lean not on your own understanding;"—that's where we put our confidence in God. "In all your ways acknowledge Him,"—that's where we prove our trustworthiness and move in faith and obedience even if we're looking at water. "And He shall direct your paths"—that's the outcome! That's where you see the waters roll back! When you and God get the trust and trustworthy concept working together like a well-oiled machine, miracles happen. I'm not telling you that God will *always* answer everything the way you want Him to, but let me say once again that God will never ever settle for anything less than what is the absolute best for me. He loves me too much for that. And He loves you too much for that too, my friend. Whatever the outcome of any circumstance or situation, you can fully trust that God believes it is for your absolute best and for His greatest glory. Can He trust you? Are you among the remnant that will be careful with the treasure of God's trust that He has placed in you? Will you walk worthy of it as a woman of God?

Sometimes our circumstances are not what we expected. I'm certain that Leah never expected to find herself an unloved bride. But she found her praise, and her heart had to trust that she was where God chose for her to be, doing what He called her to do. God can be trusted with your trust. He knows it's bruised and broken. Give it to Him anyway, and let Him help you find your praise. It's crucial! Your promises are waiting to be released!

Challenge Question

Take a moment for self-examination and simply ask yourself, "Have I proven to God that He can trust me?"

_____

_____

_____

_____

_____

_____

_____

_____

_____

_____

_____

_____

_____

_____

_____

_____

_____

_____

_____

_____

_____

Journal

CHAPTER 6

Rest

The surrendered heart of praise is at rest. Rest. Now, there's a foreign word for most of us. We have no memory of what rest feels like. Have even forgotten the definition of the word! Who has time to rest? A better question is who has the frame of mind to rest? There are so many things to think about, so many concerns, so many things to be done ... and the list continues with a plethora of things that consume every waking thought. Don't get me wrong. I'm not belittling or making light of anything that we deal with. Many of you wake up every morning facing heartbreaking situations. My heart cries with you, dear sister. But that's all the more reason that you need to understand this beautiful command from our Father God to rest.

The definition of rest is: "cease from work or movement in order to relax, refresh oneself, or recover strength, ease up/off, let up, slow down, have/take a break, unbend, unwind, recharge one's batteries, be at leisure, take it easy, put one's feet up, lie down, go to bed, take five, have/take a breather, get some shut-eye, take a load off, chill, chillax." Wow! If only, right? In a perfect world, maybe. As women, we are forced to be Superwoman, Superwife, Supermom, Super-------(you name it). And yet by God's own design for us, rest is a vital part of a healthy existence physically, mentally, emotionally, and spiritually.

So what does God have to say about rest? In Matthew 11:28 He says, "Come to me, all you who labor and are heavy laden, and I will give you rest" (NKJV). The word *rest* in this passage refers to repose and refresh.

Repose—a state of rest, sleep, or tranquility. Refresh—revitalize, revive, restore. This scripture falls toward the end of the passage concerning John the Baptist after he was thrown into prison and sent his followers to ask Jesus if He was the one they were looking for. Jesus instructed them to tell John about the miracles that He had performed and then began to rebuke the cities that had also seen these mighty works but still didn't believe. Then He utters these famous words in verse 28 about rest. Could it be that He is trying to tell us that despite our failures, despite our questions, despite any situation/circumstance, and despite the fact that we, too, have seen Him move in miraculous ways yet still doubt, He offers this rest? This place of true peace. This place to be revived and restored to the place where we were before life overwhelmed us, and we fell into this same doubt as these cities that He rebuked. To restore us to the place where we know that, yes, He is the one that we are looking for! He goes on to say in verse 29: "Take My yoke upon you and learn from me, for I am [a]gentle and lowly in heart and you will find rest for your souls" (NKJV). *Rest* here refers to cleansing. A place where, not only are we reminded of who He is but a place where the doubt, fear, despair, hopelessness … and the list goes on, is washed away, leaving the mind and spirit whole as God intended.

David seemed to understand this rest because in Psalm 16:9 he said, "Therefore my heart is glad, and my glory rejoices; my flesh also will rest in hope" (NKJV). *Rest* in this verse refers to reside or permanently dwell. *Heart* refers to the center of the feelings, the will, and the intellect. *Glad* is brightened or cheerful. *Glory* refers to weight or heaviness, and *flesh* refers to the body. *Rejoice* is to spin around under the influence of a violent emotion, and *hope* is a place of refuge, confidence, and assurance. What enabled David to grasp this deep understanding of rest? Let's back up to verse 8. "I have set the Lord always before me; Because He is at my right hand I shall not be moved" (NKJV). David was focused on his relationship with the Lord above all that was happening in the world around him. A relationship so strong that it could not be shaken by any enemy of the flesh or the spirit. A relationship that offered such assurance that God would provide all, and he needed only to dwell in His presence. So, if I may, allow me to quote this in my own words with the depths of what David is trying to say. "Therefore all that I am, all I feel and believe, my will and understanding is brightened, and my heaviness and all that weighs on me spin with the knowledge that my God is with me, and I will not be moved by any of these afflictions; my mind/body also will permanently dwell in the place of refuge and assurance." Beautiful, isn't it? That's exactly what God intends for all of us.

David also says in Psalms 116:7: "Return to your rest, O my soul, For the LORD has dealt bountifully with you" (NKJV). *Rest* in this verse is home or a settled spot. Sister, God is aware of all the things that rob you of your rest. All of it. He knows what robs you physically, emotionally, mentally, and spiritually. But He calls you to a place of rest. To return home, where you can abide in His shadow. So slow down; take a breather. Chillax! Be still, and let Him show you that He is God.

Challenge Question

What is robbing you of your rest? Be still and listen.

_____

_____

_____

_____

_____

_____

_____

_____

_____

_____

_____

_____

_____

_____

_____

_____

_____

_____

_____

_____

_____

Journal

CHAPTER 7

Presence-Minded

"So he answered and said to me: 'This is the word of the LORD to Zerubbabel: 'Not by might nor by power, but by My Spirit,' says the LORD of hosts" Zechariah 4:6 (NKJV).

If I tried to count the times in my life that I have started a prayer and immediately went into the "please do this, God" and "please do that, God," the number would be higher than man has ever been or will be able to comprehend. But a few years ago I participated in a growth/small group based on a book by Bill Johnson entitled *Hosting the Presence*. That growth group was a life changer and a prayer changer for me.

Even though it's been a few years, God is still teaching me about the power of His presence. Recently, He impressed me how much we limit His presence. Hear me out, girlfriends. We talk about a great service and say, "the presence of God was so strong." Or we just testify about our own special quiet time where we felt His presence in a special way. That's great and wonderful and there is nothing like experiencing the presence of God in a way that refreshes, renews, and brings peace. But God is teaching me that His presence accomplishes so much more and is meant for so much more than a "feel-good moment" that we limit it to. In His presence are direction, instruction, and revelation. Strongholds and obstacles are exposed in His light, and the strategy of the enemy's plan is revealed as well as our plan of attack in return.

In Zechariah 4:6, God specifically says it's not by His might or His power but by His Spirit. I have come to realize that the very presence of

God surrounding a situation, circumstance, or whatever it is changes it. Nothing can remain the same in the presence of God. We learned in our growth group that anything that is *not* created by God is not able to live in His presence. If He didn't create it, it can't breathe.

Not long ago I was fighting several battles all at the same time, and I had what I can only describe as a complete loss of sanity because I became convinced that God was clueless about all of them. I had thought about it all day and night, very carefully examined each detail of each situation, and understood exactly what should be done and explained it to God every single day. But for whatever reason that I couldn't fathom He was not taking my advice. Then one day He dropped a word into my spirit. He simply said, "Become aware of my awareness." That statement spoken directly into the midst of all of my situations changed my whole perspective. God was fully aware of every detail of everything that touched me. I could tell Him nothing that He didn't already know. The word was seemingly so simple but so powerful!

I've learned a lot about the presence of God. I've come to realize that instead of telling God every single detail of every single situation of every single person every single day, to just ask Him to surround all of it in His presence. I pray every morning with a fullness mind-set. A fullness mind-set, a least for me, is the understanding that His presence is more than the shout and the dance we experience in worship. It's the expectation that, first of all, God is aware of all the situations, and just His very presence will change it and will bring with it all the revelations, understanding, instructions, direction, and even reprimand that I need. There is not one thing that I need that cannot be met engulfed in the presence of the one who loves me more than I will ever understand or that my family needs that cannot be met engulfed in the presence of the one who loves them more than I do. I have discovered that I don't have to rehash the details every day because, after all, God doesn't forget. The presence of God is more powerful than our minds can comprehend. Don't limit what His presence can do. Don't put it in a box and only take it out when you need to feel peace or even just want to worship. Open your heart and mind, and let Him show you the fullness of His presence.

Challenge Question

Are you aware of His awareness? What holds you back?

_____

_____

_____

_____

_____

_____

_____

_____

_____

_____

_____

_____

_____

_____

_____

_____

_____

_____

_____

_____

_____

_____

Journal

CHAPTER 8

The Mourning Heart

"Blessed are those who mourn, for they shall be comforted" Matthew 5:4 (NKJV). I understand that mourning is not a state of emotion that normally connects with praise. But hear me out on this. The surrendered heart of praise is not afraid to mourn. Mourning is the act of expressing sorrow. Most of the time we associate it with death, but mourning is the emotion we feel over any loss. We just finished the previous chapter about rest. When our heart is truly in that place of rest, that refuge under the shadow of the Almighty, then that's the place of safety we need for healing. Trouble doesn't go away because we pretend it's not there; circumstances don't change because we refuse to face them, and emotions are not healed because we deny how we feel.

It's so sad that we live in a world that teaches that a show of emotion is a sign of weakness, or worse, a sign of mental instability. In my opinion, a lot of mental instability comes as a result of being afraid to show emotion for fear of being labeled as mentally incompetent. What a cycle that is! Medical science has tons of information citing how suppressed emotions affect the mind and body. Check it out sometime; it will shock you.

A couple of years ago I invited a friend of mine, a pastor's wife, to speak at an annual event I organized for our Women's Ministry. I told her to run in whatever direction God led her, and she delivered a powerful message about the right to mourn. Later, another friend at another event felt impressed to give the message that "it's okay to not be okay." God is trying to tell us something, girls. He doesn't intend for us to keep walking around in a cloud of emotional turmoil.

Since my heart is for women's ministry and, specifically, for the emotional healing of women, it disturbs me that we are not allowed to complete our cycle of mourning. I don't mean "cycle" in a negative sense here. For whatever reason, God chose to make women emotional creatures, and when we aren't given the freedom to express those emotions, we never heal. Has anyone ever told you to quit crying, get over it, and just let it go? Most of you just answered yes to all of those. So let me remind you that God gives a beautiful promise in Matthew 5:4. He says, "Blessed are those that mourn for they shall be comforted." The word *blessed* in this text refers to fortunate, happy, and well off. *Comforted* refers to "call near or invite," and in some versions of the Bible the word *comforted* even reads as "made glad." So let's read this verse again in our everyday language: "Happy are those that express sorrow, for they shall be called near and made glad." This one sentence seems to describe the whole grieving process. God is giving you permission to mourn, and you are happy and blessed if you can grasp that concept. He calls you near and invites you to climb into His lap so that He can hold you while you cry just like you do for your children. And then comes the healing. It may take awhile, but the healing process has begun.

Sister, don't let anyone strip you of your right to mourn. If God chose to include it in the Beatitudes, He obviously thought it was important. Don't let your emotions crack under the pressure of trying to hold it all in. You wouldn't push your hurting child away and deny the comfort of hiding in your arms. Neither will God deny you. He has provided a way of escape, a path toward your healing, and has granted you the right to come. He sees you suffering; He sees your tears; He hears you weeping at night, and the whole time He's been gently calling, patiently waiting for you to come to Him. Go now, dear friend. Let the tears flow, and let the healing begin.

Challenge Question

Write down anything that you've buried deep inside, and give yourself permission to grieve.

_____

_____

_____

_____

_____

_____

_____

_____

_____

_____

_____

_____

_____

_____

_____

_____

_____

_____

_____

_____

_____

Journal

CHAPTER 9

Expects, Hopes, and Waits

"Now may the God of hope fill you with all joy and peace in believing, that you may abound in hope by the power of the Holy Spirit" Romans 15:13 (NKJV). My children are grown now, but all through school my son, Andrew, had some hard struggles, battles that were really intense. Therefore, spiritual-prayer-warrior-ready-to-do-battle-soldier mom came in with both barrels blazing. My battle plan included driving by the school every single morning (and maybe again at lunch) with my hand outstretched toward the school binding every single kind of spirit I could think of that might possibly even consider coming against him. But then one morning God spoke to me. I will never forget that moment. I can even take you to the red light in my hometown where the revelation came. It started out as a question with God asking me if I knew what I was doing. "Sure, God. I'm binding spirits that might try to come against Andrew." Every single morning I woke up in battle mode, ready to defend my son, trying to identify any and all possibilities of an enemy attack. But that morning I drove to work in shame and shock when God revealed to me that I had come to expect more out of the enemy than I expected out of God. I spent most of every day letting the enemy know that I was on to him, declaring war with everything I thought Satan could think of when I should have been releasing faith, standing on the Word that tells us that grace abounds much more than sin, asking God to surround Andrew in His presence, and then just stand still and watch God work. I constantly lived in battle mode when I should have lived in victory mode. What if I had spent the day excited about what he would tell me that God had done when he got home from school instead of expecting to only hear about the struggles and whatever negativity the enemy had brought that day so I could plan my strategy for the next day? Worst of all, what did I teach Andrew about faith and expectation? What did that say about my praise?

Looking back, I have to admit that my praise was lip service. I loved the Lord with all my heart, but I would proclaim my unshakable faith in a miracle-working God and wake up every morning with determination to do things on my own and to accomplish what I didn't think God would do. It's not that He couldn't. I had no doubt in God's ability; I just doubted His willingness to move for me.

That doubt probably has something to do with the fact that I'm not really good at waiting on anything, even God. I hope I'm not the only one who struggles with that. Don't you wish God would get a new clock? One that's a little faster? If God ever decides to write about me, I can assure you it won't look anything like the book of Job. Job and I do not have much in common. On a side note here, let me give you one piece of advice: be ready if you ever pray for patience. I did that once and haven't had the nerve to do that again. However, waiting for God is essential in our everyday lives. I love Psalms 27:14: "Wait on the LORD; be of good courage, and He shall strengthen your heart; Wait, I say, on the Lord! (NKJV). Do you have any idea what the word *wait* refers to in this text? It means expect. When you've done all you know, then it's time to simply stand firm in total expectation that God will do something. It may not be what you want, but God will never just leave you hanging. And remember, sister, even if the outcome is not what you pray, it's what God decided is best for you. You might not understand it; you may question, and you may hurt, but you can rest in knowing that God is never wrong.

I'm reminded of Mary and Martha when they called for Jesus when Lazarus was sick. They expected him to come running, but he didn't get there until after Lazarus died. Don't you think they questioned why he didn't come earlier? Jesus knew they had all those questions. He knew they didn't understand, but what he also knew that they didn't was that he had something greater in mind. They had asked for a healing, but he was about to give them a resurrection! In order for it to happen, he had to let them hit rock bottom. He had to let them go through the suffering, pain, and devastation of losing their brother. Don't think for a minute that he enjoyed seeing them hurting with their hearts broken. But it was necessary so they could receive the greater miracle.

Maybe you're in that same situation. It may not be a death, but if you are facing a devastating situation, it may just be that God has a greater miracle than what you can see or what you are asking for.

We often quote Psalms 37:7: "Rest in the LORD, and wait patiently for Him" (NKJV) when we are trying to wait for God. The phrase "wait patiently" refers to "to whirl as in dancing" or to "writhe in pain." I had to process that the first time I ever studied it. How could it have two meanings completely opposite of each other? One denotes happiness, and the other denotes pain. My conclusion is that while I'm waiting on God, it's my choice how I want to spend my time. I can grumble and complain to God about why I have to endure it, and I can miss everything that God wants to teach me while I'm there. Or I can choose to dance, to keep my hope, my trust, and my expectation in my God that He will come to my rescue, and I can embrace something new that he wants to teach me.

There is power in the waiting. There is also purpose. It would be great if God would always give an immediate answer to prayer. In his wisdom, though, he doesn't always answer what I call a surface prayer. We ask for what we see in front of us, but we have no idea how it will affect everything and everyone around us. It's kind of like dropping a pebble in water. Once your rock goes under the water your attention goes to something else, but the ripples go on and on and on. God knows exactly what impact the answer to our petition will have. For example, if you ask for a job, God knows how it will affect your schedule, your family's schedule, homework and kids' activities, dinnertime, ministries you are involved in, and the list goes on. God goes into the depth of your prayer and begins to put each layer in place so that everything is ready by the time the phone rings with your job offer. When prayers are not answered immediately, we want to accuse God of delay, but we need to understand that sometimes it's not delay, its purpose. He's working on it. How will you spend the time until He gets it all prepared? Will you dance, or will you writhe in pain?

With expectation there is hope. The two go hand in hand. One of my favorite verses is Romans 15:13, which I quoted at the beginning of this chapter: ""Now may the God of hope fill you with all joy and peace in believing, that you may abound in hope by the power of the Holy Spirit" (NKJV). The word *hope* in this text refers to expectation as abstract or concrete. God is big on hope! The problem sometimes is that we get our own version of hope mixed up with God's version of hope. We say things such as, "I hope God will …," but in reality what we're saying is that "maybe God will" or "if God will." God is not an "if" or "maybe" kind of God. Second Corinthians 1:20 tells us that all the promises of God are yes and amen! "For all the promises of God in Him are Yes, and in Him Amen, to the glory of God through us" (NKJV). I'm learning to let hope become what is. That means to let hope go from an action verb to a noun. As an action verb, it's something that we do. As a noun, it means that whatever you are hoping for has come into existence and has become tangible.

It's time to change every "if God" to "when God." It's a challenge, but if you will allow it, it will completely change your mind-set. God loves you too much to be a mediocre God. He doesn't move mountains for you just because He can. He moves mountains because His love for you compels Him to. It's not what He does for you that makes Him God. It's because He's God that He moves for you in mighty ways.

Challenge Question #1

Identify every situation in your life that starts with "if God" and write it down as "when God."

_____

_____

_____

_____

_____

_____

_____

_____

_____

_____

_____

_____

_____

_____

_____

_____

_____

_____

_____

Challenge Question #2

Are you waiting on God for an answer for something? How are you spending your time?

_____

_____

_____

_____

_____

_____

_____

_____

_____

_____

_____

_____

_____

_____

_____

_____

_____

_____

_____

Journal

CHAPTER 10

Hindrances

We've examined a few characteristics of a surrendered heart of praise, but we can't leave the topic without identifying a few hindrances concocted by the enemy to keep you silent. There is a huge list, but I'm only going to include three in this study: tradition, a critical spirit, and a victim mentality.

Hindrance #1: tradition. I realize I'm on thin ice with tradition. Teachings and examples passed from generation to generation are priceless. That's what lays our spiritual foundations upon which our relationship with God is built, and what you learn from childhood until now is to be treasured, not discarded. But you have to find your own song, your own praise, and your own lifestyle of worship. Let me say this gently and lovingly. If you live the way you do, worship the way you do, pray the way you do because it's the way someone else has always lived, worshiped, and prayed, then you haven't found yours. Don't pattern your own praise or your own worship after anyone else. Do something you've never done. I am in no way suggesting that you go rogue in the next church service. But don't let fear rob you of your song. A former pastor used to talk about throwing the devil a curve ball. When everything is always the same or becomes routine, then Satan is ready for that. He knows exactly how you worship, whether it's corporate worship or your own private time, and it's easy for him to form a battle plan to distract and hinder. Anything unexpected sends him into frenzy. He's not prepared for it, and he doesn't have time to form a defense against anything outside your normal routine. It creates chaos in the enemy's camp, and while Satan and his minions scramble to find something, anything, to throw at you to stop you, breakthrough has happened! Strongholds are crumbling! For some of you the unexpected can be as simple as raising your hands or singing your prayer. (I suggest you try it.) Whatever way you choose to praise, to worship, make sure it's from *your* heart, *your* way, and *your* song.

Hindrance #2: critical spirit. Nothing gets under my skin quicker than negativity that is unleashed from the mouth of a critical spirit. I'm not talking about constructive criticism that produces a positive effect. I'm talking about the tear down, destroy, hurt, and kill kind of criticism. How many scriptures are there about the untamed tongue, telling us that the mouth speaks from whatever is in the heart, and then give specific guidelines on what to think about so we speak about? Remember Philippians 4:8–9? "Finally, brethren, whatever things are true, whatever things are noble, whatever things are just, whatever things are pure, whatever things are lovely, whatever things are of good report, if there is any virtue and if there is anything praiseworthy—meditate on these things. The things which you learned and received and heard and saw in me, these do, and the God of peace will be with you." (NKJV). There is a reason for these instructions. God hates negativity. I have learned that God will reprimand, discipline, and reveal truth that I may not want to hear, but He has never, ever, and will never, ever, use criticism for correction. Negative words to God are like nails on a chalkboard. If He saw the need to call it out in His Word, then He doesn't intend for it to be a part of your personality.

Remember a few chapters ago when I referred to the children of Israel on the banks of the Red Sea? I pointed out that only a remnant in that group would make it to the Promised Land. Do remember what their problem was? The Bible says they started to murmur and complain. Have you ever thought about why this is dangerous? I admit that I never really had until I heard a minister friend touch on it in a message. Murmuring and complaining is deadly to the spiritual life. Once that mind-set takes root, it smothers out the ability to see any good in anyone or anything; it stumps any growth of that person; it creates an atmosphere of complete negativity and spills over into church and family so that there is no growth there either. I could go on with a list of effects, but in a nutshell it's this: it brings a person to a place where he or she becomes unteachable. Once a person is to that point, he or she begins to reject anything that God is doing. Take notice of your words, sisters. Proceed with caution.

Hindrance #3: victim mentality. This is the last one I will address. Many of you have suffered some serious things, and I'm not at all belittling the pain you still suffer as a result. But hear this, daughter of God. He doesn't intend for you to live in that place anymore. Some people, especially women, use their situation as an excuse for everything. It becomes a crutch when needed or a trump card to be played when she finds herself in an uncomfortable place. Remember Joseph? Remember all the things he endured? Remember what he said to his brothers decades later when they all reunited again in Egypt? Look at Genesis 50:20. Joseph declares that what was intended as evil against him, God used for good. "But as for you, you meant evil against me; but God meant it for good" (NKJV). This is what I believe God wants to speak to someone right now. Evil came against you, but if you will shed the victim clothing, God will use it for His glory. He will turn your mess into a message!

Challenge Question #1

What hinders your worship? Be honest. Write down your strategy for freedom.

_____

_____

_____

_____

_____

_____

_____

_____

_____

_____

_____

_____

_____

_____

_____

_____

_____

_____

_____

_____

_____

Challenge Question #2

Write you own psalm of praise.

_____

_____

_____

_____

_____

_____

_____

_____

_____

_____

_____

_____

_____

_____

_____

_____

_____

_____

_____

_____

_____

Challenge Question #3

Read Philippians 4:8–9. Do your words fall outside of these guidelines?

_____

_____

_____

_____

_____

_____

_____

_____

_____

_____

_____

_____

_____

_____

_____

_____

_____

_____

_____

_____

_____

CHAPTER 11

The Other Veils

Jacob looks at his bride with great anticipation. Rachel. His true love. The one he has waited for. Now she is his. His bride, the future mother of his children. And all that separates him from her, all that keeps him from looking into her eyes, touching her beautiful face, is the veil. Slowly he walks over to her, love shining in his eyes. Slowly his hands reach out and gently grasp the edges of the veil, and slowly the veil begins to move. And Leah cringes. She closes her eyes, fighting back the tears, and braces for his reaction.

I can only determine two ways for which a veil is useful. One, it protects. Actually, from all indications, that seems to be the reason for the invention of the veil in the first place. It protected the one who wore it from bugs and outside elements. Two, it provides a hiding place. My guess is that that's the purpose it served for Leah, and I doubt that she wanted to leave her hiding place. Behind the veil she could be someone else. Behind the veil she was good enough and met expectations. But hiding behind the veil would keep her from her destiny. She hadn't read the rest of the story. She had no idea that she would bear a son that she would call Praise (Judah) and that through her praise a promise would be released. A promise of the Messiah that would be a Savior for the whole world for every generation. A Savior that would conquer death, hell, and the grave. She didn't know. So, she cringed behind the veil dreading the moment when her hiding place was gone, and her true identity, her flaws, and her deception were exposed, and she must face reality.

In the temple a few centuries ago, there was another veil: a veil that separated man from the presence of God. Only the high priest was allowed to enter and even then it was only once a year. Only one man. Only one day. And it wasn't a "come as you are" kind of setting. He went through cleansing rituals, and even his robes had to be specifically designed. But then something happened.

The promise that came through Leah's praise hung on a cross. And all of our sins, the baggage that comes with it, and all that separates us from God was nailed to the cross with Him. The moment, the very moment, that our separation from God was complete, the veil that covered the Holy of Holies, the veil that never allowed a personal relationship between God and man, was ripped in half. Another favorite scripture is Hebrews 4:16: "Let us therefore come boldly to the throne of grace that we may obtain mercy and find grace to help in time of need" (NKJV). God went to great lengths to remove the veil to bring life to this promise. He discarded the veil knowing that many would reject Him and would refuse the love and the life He offered. But the veil came off anyway.

That brings us to the last veil. Yours. You identify with Leah. Jesus is looking at you with more love than your mind can comprehend. He longs to look into your eyes, touch your face, and live in relationship with you. He longs to fill your heart with praise because He alone knows the promises that will be unlocked through a surrendered life of worship. Only the veil you wear separates Him from you. He comes to you, but you cringe behind your veil, safe in your hiding place even as you hear him call your name and whisper His love to you. You can't stand the disappointment, the disapproval, the rejection once He knows the real you. So your heart beats fast; you fight the tears and the desire to take a chance, and you remain in the darkness of your veil. Unlike Jacob, Jesus knows your true identity. He is fully aware of all the things in your past. But still He comes. He is aware that someone has told you that you aren't good enough. But still He comes. He is aware that someone has told you that you are worthless. But still He comes. He is fully aware of every lie that the enemy has spoken into your life. But still He comes. Still He reaches for the edges of the veil.

Come out of hiding, dear friend. He wants to replace your veil with a crown! It's time for you to live as the Lord's beloved. Remember he went to great lengths to allow you to come as you are into His presence. No pretense. Just you. Surrendered, with your heart singing a new song of praise.

Did you hear that? It's the sound of chains breaking because you just released your promise.

Challenge Question

Read Hebrews 4:16. What does it mean to you?

_____

_____

_____

_____

_____

_____

_____

_____

_____

_____

_____

_____

_____

_____

_____

_____

_____

_____

_____

_____

_____

_____

Journal

_____

_____

_____

_____

_____

_____

_____

_____

_____

_____

_____

_____

_____

_____

_____

_____

_____

_____

_____

_____

_____

_____

_____

_____

Darlene Vice

ABOUT THE AUTHOR

Darlene Vice is a retired mother of two adult children, Alicyn and Andrew. Upon retirement in 2018, after a thirty-year career with the State of Alabama, she decided to pursue her lifelong dream of writing. She and her husband of thirty-three years, Tommy, have served in their local church in many areas, in youth camps, and in other Alabama Church of God of Prophecy events. In the past, she has codirected the Church of God of Prophecy Alabama Women's Conference, and she currently serves as director of Women's Ministry at the Community Church at Hackleburg, Hackleburg, Alabama. She and Tommy reside in Detroit, Alabama.

ABOUT THE BOOK

Behind Leah's Veil examines the emotional turmoil of Leah as the marriage veil was removed revealing her true identity to an unsuspecting Jacob. After trying desperately to win his love, even choosing names for her first three sons that echo the longing in her heart, she gave birth to the fourth son, declaring that she is going to praise the Lord, and named him Judah. Through her praise, a promise is released—the Messiah. Each chapter describes a characteristic of a surrendered heart of praise and offers assurance to all women that their promises will also be released with a true lifestyle of worship.

Printed in the United States
By Bookmasters